Did Yo...

LEICEST...
& RUTLAND

A MISCELLANY

Compiled by Julia Skinner

With particular reference to the work of Michael Kilburn,
David Jones and Matt Howling

THE FRANCIS FRITH COLLECTION

www.francisfrith.com

First published in the United Kingdom in 2012 by The Francis Frith Collection®

This edition published exclusively for Identity Books in 2012 ISBN 978-1-84589-682-9

Text and Design copyright The Francis Frith Collection®
Photographs copyright The Francis Frith Collection® except where indicated.

The Frith® photographs and the Frith® logo are reproduced under licence from
Heritage Photographic Resources Ltd, the owners of the Frith® archive and trademarks.
'The Francis Frith Collection', 'Francis Frith' and 'Frith' are registered trademarks of
Heritage Photographic Resources Ltd.

British Library Cataloguing in Publication Data

Did You Know? Leicestershire & Rutland - A Miscellany
Compiled by Julia Skinner
With particular reference to the work of Michael Kilburn, David Jones and Matt Howling

The Francis Frith Collection
Oakley Business Park,
Wylye Road, Dinton,
Wiltshire SP3 5EU
Tel: +44 (0) 1722 716 376
Email: info@francisfrith.co.uk
www.francisfrith.com

Printed and bound in Malaysia
Contains material sourced from responsibly managed forests

Front Cover: **MARKET HARBOROUGH, THE OLD GRAMMAR SCHOOL 1922** 72269p
Frontispeice: **MELTON MOWBRAY, NOTTINGHAM STREET c1960** M60114
Contents: **OAKHAM, HIGH STREET 1927** 80284

The colour-tinting is for illustrative purposes only, and is not intended to be historically accurate

CONTENTS

INTRODUCTION

To many outsiders, Leicestershire is either to be slept through on a train into or out of St Pancras Station, or driven through at high speed on the M1 motorway. It is, in fact, an area worthy of special notice, a multi-faceted county of heavy Triassic claylands in the east and rocky granite and slate outcrops in the west.

The Soar Valley slices the county into two more or less equal halves, and makes Leicester the place where many old roads and tracks meet. Geographically, the city of Leicester can be compared to the hub of a wheel; its spokes are the roads and railways that link with the towns around it. Towns like Melton Mowbray, Market Harborough, Loughborough, Ashby and Lutterworth have strong agricultural roots, whilst other places like Hinckley and Coalville have an air of industry and commerce.

To insiders, The Shires are evocative worlds, conjuring up an image of rolling grasslands and sheep, with nucleated villages evenly spaced across the Ordnance Survey map, often linked by straight hawthorn-lined enclosure roads, green drove roads or more ancient ways, quickly proving the old adage that you are rarely out of sight of a church spire – Leicestershire has some wonderful examples of these, and the needle-like spire which crowns the pink granite tower of St Mary's Church at Queniborough is said by Pevsner to be one of the finest in the county (see photograph Q12001, opposite).

Under the grassland, history is preserved in the familiar 'medieval' ridge-and-furrow patterns of selions and furlongs. It is interesting that the patterns are generally referred to as medieval – although recent archaeological evidence points, in some places, to a pre-Conquest date, the remains as we see them must have been in use immediately before the late 18th- or early 19th-century enclosures.

Many years ago Leicestershire became a centre for foxhunting, especially around Quorn, Belvoir, Melton Mowbray and Market Harborough, and farmers created special woodlands as cover for foxes that are still part of the landscape today.

Rutland's motto means 'much in little', which is very apt for this unspoilt gem of English countryside and the smallest county in England, which in 1997 was restored as a county in its own right, after the unpopular local government reorganisation of 1974 which merged it with Lincolnshire.

QUENIBOROUGH, THE VILLAGE AND ST MARY'S CHURCH c1955
Q12001

DIALECT WORDS AND PHRASES FROM LEICESTERSHIRE & RUTLAND

'Bungole' – cheese.

'Are kid' or **'mi chip'** – my brother.

'Charlie's dead' – your petticoat is showing.

'Coddie' – foreman.

'Cotty' – tangled or untidy hair.

'The cut' – the canal.

'Duck's necks' – bottles of fizzy drinks.

'E's gorra chin on' – he's being sulky, or cross.

'Ginnel' – an alleyway or path.

'I ain't up Co'ville' – I can hear you, no need to shout.

'Jollop' – medicine.

'Mashin the tea' – brewing the tea.

'Necky Becky' – a nosey person.

'Puthering down with rain' – raining very heavily.

'Skants' – underwear.

'Snaps' – lunch, or a snack.

'Well, I'll go to the foot of our stairs' – that's really surprised me.

UPPINGHAM, LONDON ROAD, 1922 72285x

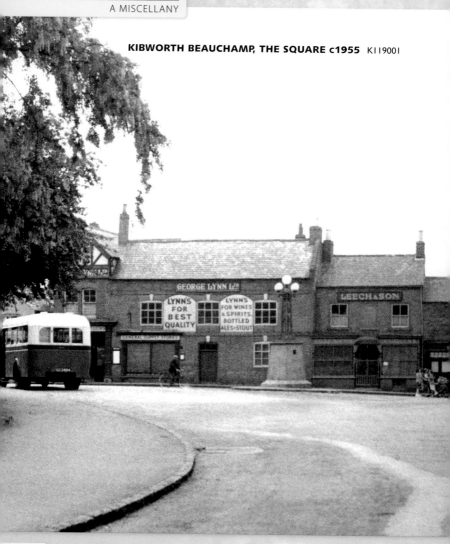

KIBWORTH BEAUCHAMP, THE SQUARE c1955 K119001

HAUNTED LEICESTERSHIRE

There are many ghost stories associated with Leicester. The city's most haunted building is said to be the Guildhall, which boasts five ghosts (see photograph L144025, page 14). The most frequent visitor, though rarely seen, has been dubbed the White Lady, who moves heavy furniture around the library, and opens locked doors. The Abbey Pumping Station is said to be haunted by the ghost of an engineer who fell to his death from the top balcony into the engine room in the 19th century. Staff at Newarke Houses Museum have reported feeling the presence of someone nearby and visitors are told to look out for a glimpse of a mysterious cloaked figure. In 1998 Belgrave Hall was the scene of a paranormal investigation after two figures in Victorian clothing were spotted on CCTV. They seemed to have come through a courtyard wall. Investigators concluded that the images had been caused by falling leaves – but who knows…

The Black Dog Inn in Oadby is said to have its own ghost, possibly linked to an earlier use of the Long Skittle Alley as a morgue.

Legend has it that a miller who lived at Kibworth, just outside Market Harborough, died after being buried alive and his ghost came back to haunt local people. The story goes that the miller had been drinking large quantities of gin for a bet in the now-demolished Coach and Horses Inn, but to ensure he lost, his friends made all his drinks doubles. He drank them all and won, but fell down unconscious afterward. He was proclaimed dead and duly buried. However, there were later suspicions that he might not have been dead and had been buried alive; some witnesses said they heard noises coming from his coffin, and there were stories that his spectre had been seen in the area …

LEICESTERSHIRE & RUTLAND MISCELLANY

What is now Leicester was once the 'civitas', or capital, of a Celtic tribe, and was called Ratae Coritanorum by the Romans, who had an important settlement here. The remains of Ratae Coritanorum lie adjacent to the Saxon church of St Nicholas (one of the oldest churches in England) and are seen in the centre of photograph L144069 (opposite). Also shown in the photograph is the so-called Jewry Wall, believed to date from AD130, which formed part of the exercise hall to the public baths of the Roman town.

After the Norman Conquest a castle was built at Leicester, but it was destroyed in 1173 during a rebellion against Henry II; despite a later rebuilding, all that survives is the motte and the Great Hall, which dates from the late 12th century. It has been pared down from its original aisled form, and provided with what is basically a 17th-century range and brick front. It is now used as the Crown Court.

The name of Leicester's De Montfort Hall commemorates Simon de Montfort, the 1st Earl of Leicester, who led a successful revolt of the barons against Henry III. The Parliament that de Montfort summoned in 1265 set a precedent for future relations between the English monarch and subjects.

Leicester's Newarke Houses Museum is composed of two historic houses, Wygston's Chantry House and Skeffington House. Wygston's Chantry House was built c1511-12 by William Wygston, in his day Leicester's wealthiest citizen. It was the home of two chantry priests who sang masses for William's soul in the nearby (now demolished) church of St Mary of the Annunciation. The house was restored in the 1950s, after war damage, and is the only Elizabethan urban gentry house that survives in Leicestershire.

LEICESTER, THE ROMAN REMAINS AND JEWRY WALL c1955
L144069

Photograph L144097 (below) shows Leicester's Gothic Clock Tower, which was designed by local architect Joseph Goddard in 1868. It is decorated with pinnacles and canopies, along with representations of four Leicester worthies: Alderman Gabriel Newton, Simon de Montfort, William Wygston and Sir Thomas White, one-time Mayor of Leicester and landlord of the nearby Horse and Trumpet.

**LEICESTER, THE CLOCK TOWER
AND GALLOWTREE GATE
c1965** L144097

A plaque on Bow Bridge at Leicester records a prophecy given to Richard III as he rode over the bridge on his way to his death at the Battle of Bosworth in 1485. Richard's spur struck the parapet, and a bystander predicted that his head would later do the same. The prophecy came true two days later, when the king's body was brought back to Leicester, dangling across a horse's back – and his head did indeed hit the parapet. The king's body is believed to have been buried in the chapel of the Grey Friars. Legend says that his bones were dug up at the Dissolution of the Monasteries in the 16th century and thrown over Bow Bridge, later to be buried on the banks of the Soar, and that a stone coffin, said to be the king's, was used as a horse trough at the White Horse Inn, Gallowtree Gate.

The name of Gallowtree Gate in Leicester probably refers to the gallows which were sited at the top of London Road hill, close to its junction with Evington Lane.

Leicester was the venue in 1426 of the intriguingly named Parliament of Bats. The king at the time, Henry VI, was an infant, and there was great tension between the Duke of Gloucester, the king's uncle and regent, and Cardinal Beaufort, the Bishop of Winchester. The members were forbidden by the Duke of Gloucester to carry swords into the parliament, but were so concerned that violent disagreement might ensue that they armed themselves with clubs, or bats – hence the name.

The Abbey of St Mary de Pratis in Leicester, which is laid out in the north-west angle of Abbey Park, was one of the largest in England of the Augustinian Order but was dissolved in 1538. Cardinal Wolsey, who fell from grace over the matter of Henry VIII's divorce from Catherine of Aragon, died at the abbey in 1530, whilst travelling to London to answer charges of treason. A slab in Abbey Park marks the presumed site of his grave.

LEICESTER, GRANBY STREET 1949 L144032

Leicester is famous for its Victorian architecture. Some of the superb buildings of this period are the HSBC Bank in the city centre (on the corner of Granby Street and Bishop Street), the Turkey Café (in Granby Street, opposite Bishop Street), and the former Singer Building in the High Street (now 76-88 Coronation Building). The HSBC Bank is adorned with monsters which crawl over the walls; these are the work of the stonemason Samuel Barfield, who often worked with the architect of the building, Joseph Goddard, who also designed the Clock Tower and the Thomas Cook Building in Leicester. The Turkey Café building features a number of portrayals of turkeys, on either side of the entrance and in a mosaic on the top floor. The architect was Arthur Wakerley, who later became Mayor of Leicester, who also designed the Singer Building.

Every Street in Leicester got its name from a carrier (an early haulage/taxi business) who had a notice on the wall there claiming that he could take you to 'every street in Leicester'.

A Market Harborough cabinet-maker named Thomas Cook organized the first ever railway excursion. Cook had a deep interest in evangelical work and in 1834, while walking from Harborough to Leicester, he came up with the idea of using the railway to transport a large number of people from Leicester to Loughborough to a religious rally. He persuaded the railway company that the scheme would be profitable, and went on to become world famous as the founder of the travel agents Thomas Cook & Son, which he started from a building in Leicester overlooking the Clock Tower (seen immediately to the left of the Clock Tower in photograph L144097 on page 10).

Even before the Industrial Revolution, Leicester had a thriving hosiery industry. In the 1720s Daniel Defoe noted: 'Leicester is an ancient, large and populous town … They have considerable manufacture carried on here, and in several of the market towns round for weaving of stockings by frames, and one would scarce think it possible so small an article of trade could employ such multitudes of people as it does; for the whole county seems to be employed in it.' However, Leicester's development into the industrial city of today was due to the construction of the Grand Union Canal in the 1790s, linking Leicester to London and Birmingham, and the coming of the railway in the 19th century. The hosiery industry flourished, and Leicester continued to expand, aided by the successful boot- and shoe-making and engineering industries – in 1831, 425 boot and shoemakers were recorded in the city; by 1861 there were 2,741. Several household names had factories in the city, among them Freeman, Hardy & Willis, and George Oliver.

Leicester is home to the Leicestershire Museum of Technology, which features a collection of 19th-century beam pumping engines; these can be seen working on 'steaming' days. There is also the largest collection of hosiery machinery in the world, reflecting the importance of that industry to the county in the past.

Leicester grew rapidly in the 18th and 19th centuries, but until 1876 it continued to be governed from its small medieval Guildhall (photograph L144025, below). A visit to the Guildhall is well worthwhile, to see the amazing 14th-century timbered Great Hall of the Corpus Christi Guild, a powerful guild of local businessmen and gentry. The Corporation bought the building in 1548 when the Guild was dissolved. Since then the Guildhall has had many uses, and survived calls for its demolition as an eyesore in the early 20th century, but is now in safe hands as a performance venue and museum. Visitors to the Guildhall Museum will find 'Crankie Gemmie' and 'Emma Smith', two of Leicester's notorious pickpockets, languishing in the Victorian police cells.

LEICESTER, THE GUILDHALL, GUILDHALL LANE c1949 L144025

St Martin's Church in Leicester was raised to cathedral status in 1927. Its magnificent East Window is a monument to the dead of the First World War; its design makes much use of red, which sets the cathedral ablaze when the morning light streams through it. In the centre, Jesus is portrayed holding a starry heaven in his hand, whilst his foot rests on a bloody hell; around Him stand 8 angels, whose wings are depicted in red glass. The window also depicts St Martin, to whom the cathedral is dedicated, standing on the tail of a dragon, with St George standing on its head. A First World War soldier can also be found. The window is particularly significant in this cathedral, as the saint day of St Martin, the patron saint of the cathedral, is 11th November, Armistice Day.

There are two war memorials in Leicester's Victoria Park. Best known is the Memorial Arch, which commemorates the First World War and was designed by the great architect Sir Edwin Lutyens. The second memorial commemorates the American 82nd Airborne Division, who were based in Leicester prior to the D Day landings in 1944.

Leicester is moving forward into the 21st century as a vibrant modern city with a large immigrant population. Life in Leicester has been greatly enriched by the diversity of the festivals and cultures of its citizens, such as the Diwali lights, the Caribbean Carnival and the fruit and vegetables from all over the world that can be found at Leicester Market, the largest covered market in Europe. Leicester is particularly famous for its renowned Indian restaurants, many of which are to be found along Belgrave Road.

LEICESTER, ST MARTIN'S CATHEDRAL c1955 L144026

'Harborough' in the name of Market Harborough derives from the Anglo-Saxon 'Haeferabeorg', meaning 'the hill where oats are grown'. It was the name of a field used by the men of Bowden and Arden, which is now Mill Hill.

The name of Gartree in Market Harborough dates back to ancient times when criminals were executed by hanging at the 'Gallow-tree', just outside the town. Over time, the name 'Gallow-tree' slowly became 'Gar-tree'. It is now the site of Gartree Prison, which was the scene of a dramatic breakout in December 1987, when two prisoners, killer Sydney Draper and gang boss John Kendall, were lifted to freedom by helicopter from the jail's exercise yard.

MARKET HARBOROUGH, THE MARKET PLACE 1922 72264

MARKET HARBOROUGH, THE OLD GRAMMAR SCHOOL 1922

Robert Smyth was Market Harborough's very own version of Dick Whittington, a poor boy who left Harborough for London around 1570 to seek his fortune, and found work as an archivist for the Lord Mayor's Court. He became very successful, eventually becoming Comptroller of the City of London, but he always remembered the place where he was 'bred and fed'. Smyth often sent money up from London to provide bread for the 'godly honest poor' of the town, which would be handed out on the Sabbath day. But he is most remembered today for founding the Old Grammar School in Harborough's Market Place in 1614 (see photograph 72269, above). Built on posts 'to keep people dry in times of foul weather' and to allow the butter market to be held on the ground floor, it is one of the town's best-known landmarks. The Old Grammar School was in use as a school until 1909.

**MARKET HARBOROUGH
ST DIONYSIUS CHURCH
1922** 72267

A former pupil of the Old Grammar School in Market Harborough, Sir William Bragg, and his son, Lawrence Bragg, were jointly awarded the Nobel Prize for Physics in 1915 for their pioneering work in creating a new branch of science called crystallography. This was the analysis of crystal structures using X-rays.

The Battle of Naseby, one of the turning points of the Civil War, was fought just south of Market Harborough on June 14th 1645. Oliver Cromwell wrote a famous letter from the Bell Inn in the town (now in Northampton Road) to Parliament, telling them about the battle and the Parliamentary force's victory. Cromwell's men captured members of the defeated Royalist army and imprisoned them in Harborough's St Dionysius Church, one of the town's most secure buildings (see photograph 72267, above).

Every year a traditional ceremony is held over William Hubbard's grave in the grounds of the ruined St Mary in Arden Church in Market Harborough. Hubbard was a gardener who died in 1786. He left the sum of one guinea (£1.05) a year, forever, to the singers of Market Harborough's church, on the condition that they sang a hymn every Easter Eve over his grave.

The tradition of 'bottle kicking' takes place each year just outside Market Harborough, between the villages of Hallaton and Medbourne, and dates back 1,000 years to medieval times. The aim of the annual event is to wrestle a small keg of ale back to your parish. Part of the tradition involves throwing hare pie into the crowds. This is because in medieval times a piece of land was left to the local rector on the condition that he provided hare pies, ale and loaves 'to be scrambled for' on each succeeding Easter Monday at the place called Hare Pie Bank.

The name of Loughborough is well-known all over the world. This small market town has a university with a reputation for excellence and sports; it is home to the largest bell foundry in the world; cranes and hoists designed and built in Loughborough at the Empress Works of Herbert Morris Ltd have been employed from the docks of New Jersey in the USA to the shipyards of Korea; and turbines, trams and transporters have all been made at the Falcon Works of the Brush Electrical Engineering Company.

LOUGHBOROUGH, MARKET PLACE c1955
L197019

19

**LOUGHBOROUGH
HIGH STREET 1955**
L197003

George Main is said to have been the first man to drive a motorcar in Loughborough. In 1897 he drove a Benz car, which had tiller steering (no steering wheel). The people of the town lined the streets to see this strange horseless carriage.

Only two buildings in Loughborough merit a mention in the Leicestershire & Rutland volume of Pevsner's 'Buildings of England'. All Saints' Church is perhaps to be expected, but the other entry may come as a surprise to many who know the town well. It is the original part of the Shelthorpe estate – this was built in the 1930s and was visited by town planners from all over Europe as one of the finest examples of modern urban planning. The designer was Barry Parker, who had designed the famous Hampstead Garden Suburb and Letchworth. Pevsner calls particular attention to the layout and to the 'slate hung oriels' of some of the house fronts around the central 'circus'.

21

**LOUGHBOROUGH,
THE CARILLION
QUEEN'S PARK
c1960** L197069

Taylors Bell Foundry in Loughborough was founded by John Taylor, who arrived in the town in 1839 to recast the bells of the parish church. He found conditions in Loughborough suitable to his craft, and established a foundry in Pack Horse Lane before moving the foundry to its present site in Freehold Street. In 1881 Taylors produced the country's largest bell, which hangs in St Paul's Cathedral in London; it is steam-driven and is called 'Great Paul'. It weighs over 16 tons and it took two huge traction engines to transport it from the Leicestershire foundry to London.

When the First World War ended in 1918, Loughborough had lost more than 400 of its sons. The grief and mourning of the local people found expression in a manner which is unique in England – the sound of bells, particularly appropriate to the town because of its tradition of bell founding. Loughborough's unique memorial to its war dead is a campanile in Queen's Park, a free-standing bell tower known as the Carillion (photograph L197069, opposite). Loughborough's Carillion has 47 bells of different sizes, giving it a wide range of musical notes and allowing it to play tunes of all kinds. It is not automated and relies on the skill of the human player at its keyboard to produce its melodies. The bells in the Loughborough Carillion all have inscriptions about the donors, and there is especially poignancy for Taylors because the biggest bell was given by Edmund Denison Taylor, the head of the bell foundry, in memory of his three nephews, all killed in action in the First World War. The sound of the bells reaches out not only over the park but also across the town itself. Loughborough's Carillion is not only a memorial to the fallen in war but a living part of the town's cultural heritage.

What is now Victory Lane in Loughborough was originally known as Dead Lane – it was renamed after the First World War. It was long thought that the old name of Dead Lane was linked to an outbreak of plague in the town, but it now seems more likely that the lane was the path that led to the lychgate of the parish church, and was the route followed by funerary processions.

Oliver Cromwell's personal chaplain came from Loughborough – he was John Howe, born in the town in 1630, and he is commemorated in the name of Howe Road in Shelthorpe. Howe was famous for the length of his sermons, and is said on one occasion to have preached non-stop for more than two hours!

The fountain in Loughborough's Market Place is known as Fearon's Fountain (photograph L197703, opposite). It is named after Henry Fearon, the rector of All Saints' Church, who campaigned for many years to bring a clean supply of water to the town. He is also remembered in the name of Fearon Road in the town. The fountain originally had metal cups attached by chains to enable passers-by to have instant access to the clean water. No water flows from Fearon's Fountain now, but he remains one of the town's most fondly remembered inhabitants. When he died in 1885 the people of Loughborough lined the streets to pay their last respects, and it was written of him that 'he loved Loughborough, and Loughborough loved him'.

The famous 18th-century agricultural improver Robert Bakewell farmed at Dishley Grange near Loughborough. He was a stockbreeder, pioneering first the longhorn cattle breed (whose milk was originally used to make Stilton Cheese) and later the famous Leicester sheep, which became the basis for many modern breeds and flocks.

Market Rasen became the main market for a wide area in the 16th century, and changed its name from East to Market Rasen. The old Town Hall is seen in photograph M231002 (page 26-27) in the 1950s, when it was being used as a cinema; the building was situated in the Market Place where The Square Café Bar is now. The old Town Hall was demolished in the 1960s and a Co-op was built on the site – in the words of the Market Rasen Mail, 'an architectural disgrace that would never be allowed to happen today'.

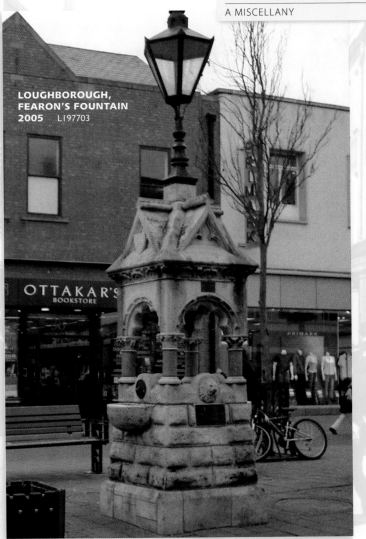

LOUGHBOROUGH,
FEARON'S FOUNTAIN
2005   L197703

MARKET RASEN, TOWN HALL CINEMA c1955 M231002

On the banks of the River Eye in north Leicestershire stands Melton Mowbray, an historic market town renowned for its famous pork pie. Melton market was the only one in Leicestershire significant enough to be recorded in the Domesday Book in 1086, by which time it was already well established. Local legend has it that the market received a Royal Charter from King Edward the Confessor in the days when Leofric ruled the Anglo-Saxon kingdom of Mercia (in which Melton was sited) with his wife, the famous Lady Godiva.

In Tudor times the Swan Inn in Melton Mowbray's Market Place was the most important building in the town after the church. It was the main inn, the venue for important business meetings, the town jail, and where the town's armour was kept (in the kitchen!). In Georgian and Regency times local balls and assemblies were held here. The Swan Inn closed in 1825 and was converted into shops, but is remembered in the Old White Swan figurine, which can be seen above Dolland & Aitcheson today (in the 1930s photograph below it can be seen on the right of the view, above W H Pearce, Outfitters). The swan figurine has an interesting place in the town's history – see opposite.

MELTON MOWBRAY, THE MARKET PLACE 1932 85169

MELTON MOWBRAY, NOTTINGHAM STREET c1960 M60114

The expression 'to paint the town red' is said to have originated in Melton Mowbray. In 1837 the Marquis of Waterford was joined by a party of friends for the Croxton Park races and the group ran riot around the town for several nights, running rings around the local constabulary and antagonising the local population with their exploits. They broke the toll gates, wrenched off door knockers, threw the sign of the Red Lion into the canal and smeared everything in sight with red paint. The Marquis of Waterford personally painted the Old White Swan figurine red as a grand finale.

Melton Mowbray is known for its world-famous pork pie, which originated here in 1831. The town was within reach of many Shire foxhunting packs and Edward Adcock, who ran a bakery in Leicester Street, made cold meat pies which proved very popular among the foxhunting fraternity as a dish served at high teas after a long day's hunting. He decided to market his pies in London, and by 1840 the increased demand was such that Enoch Evans set up a rival business in the Beast Market (now Sherrard Street), and the popularity of the Melton Mowbray pork pie began to grow. These hand-raised pies are uniquely rounded, made from the finest British uncured pork, and encased in rich and crunchy pastry. Dickinson and Morris, who run Ye Olde Pork Pie Shoppe in Nottingham Street, are the last remaining firm in Melton to bake the authentic pies on their shop premises (seen on the right of photograph M60114, above). The bakery is a huge tourist attraction, with as many as 250,000 visitors each year.

**MELTON MOWBRAY
ST MARY'S CHURCH
1927** 80308

Stilton Cheese developed in the villages east of Melton Mowbray. It became famous when Mrs Frances Pawlett, a dairywoman who lived near Melton Mowbray, made a business arrangement with Cooper Thornhill, who agreed to market her cheese. Thornhill owned the Bell Inn at Stilton in Cambridgeshire, a staging post for people travelling along the road between London and York. He introduced the cheese to travellers at the inn, and its popularity spread rapidly. The cheese took its name from the town, despite the fact that it has never actually been made in Stilton. Stilton is one of the few cheeses granted a 'protected designation of origin' status by the European Commission. This means that there are strict codes for the quality of the cheese, and it can only be made in the counties of Leicestershire, Derbyshire or Nottinghamshire, but with three main producers in the town, Melton Mowbray can claim to be the Stilton capital.

As well as Stilton, Leicestershire is also famous for Red Leicester Cheese, with a colour that ranges from russet to deep red. It was originally coloured with carrot or beet juice, but nowadays annatto extract is used.

The church of St Mary the Virgin in Melton Mowbray is one of the most impressive parish churches in Leicestershire. The oldest part of the church is the lower section of the tower, thought to date from the 12th century. The majority of the church, in the decorated style, dates from the late 13th and early 14th centuries. St Mary's is one of only five churches in England with aisled transepts, usually only seen in cathedrals. Lying in a recess of the south wall is the figure of a crusader. The inscription on the figure dates it to 1150, although evidence suggests that 1303 is a more likely date. On the east aisle of the south transept are a number of tombs and monuments. One raised tomb is that of Edward and Katherine Pate, who died in the 1590s. Their life-size figures are represented in Elizabethan dress and lie side by side. Another tomb is that of a lady of the Burgeis family, showing a woman in 14th-century dress, which is exceptionally well preserved.

NEWTOWN LINFORD, BRADGATE PARK, THE RUINS c1960 N96334

Bradgate Park near Newton Linford was enclosed out of Charnwood Forest c1200 as a hunting park. Bradgate House was built in the park using bricks produced on the site; started around 1490 by Thomas Grey, 1st Marquis of Dorset, it was Leicestershire's first true country house and was the birthplace and childhood home of Lady Jane Grey, the tragic nine-days Queen of England, who was executed in 1554. The house fell into ruin after the 1730s (photograph N96334, above).

Woodhouse Eaves, situated in the heart of the ancient forest of Charnwood, first appears as 'Wodehuses', literally meaning 'the houses in the woods', around 1210. With its close neighbour, Swithland, it is associated with a vast output of slate during the 18th and 19th centuries, which was used for roofing material and for graveyard headstones. Its ability to take the most intricate of carving and to weather it well put it among the most popular of materials, to such an extent that almost every churchyard in the county can show examples.

One of Leicestershire's hidden treasures is the magnificent 13th-century east window in the church at Twycross, thought to be the oldest stained glass window in England. It originally came from the Saint-Chapelle in Paris; it was removed for safe-keeping during the French Revolution and presented to George III; in time it was inherited by William IV who gave it to Lord Howe, and he had it installed in the church at Twycross. The window is a breathtaking example of the French stained-glass artists' work.

Ashby-de-la-Zouch had its castle immortalised as the scene of the tournament in Sir Walter Scott's 'Ivanhoe'. The castle held Mary, Queen of Scots as a prisoner for some time during her long period of captivity during the reign of Elizabeth I.

The large commuter village of Glenfield, on the north-west outskirts of Leicester, has the world's first railway tunnel, which is just over a mile long.

ASHBY-DE-LA-ZOUCH, THE CASTLE FROM ST HELEN'S CHURCH
c1965 A212029

FOXTON, THE GRAND UNION CANAL c1960 F159006

Photograph F159006 (above) shows the lock keepers' cottages at Foxton, which served the flight on the section of the Grand Union Canal known as the Leicester line. Behind the trees is the Foxton inclined plane, a late 19th-century engineering feat that lifted loaded barges up the hillside in a cradle. When the canal was first built here between 1808-14, a narrow boat trip through the ten locks would take about one hour. Because of the length of time it took to go through the locks, an inclined plane was built between 1897-1900, which raised or lowered the narrowboats from one end to the other in under ten minutes. By about 1930 this amazing piece of machinery was in a state of disuse and the metal parts were sold as scrap. The Foxton Inclined Plane Trust has now been formed to restore and care for this important part of our heritage.

Since the 18th century the town of Mountsorrel has been the birthplace of numberless pink granite setts and kerb-stones; these were originally produced for the turnpike road, but some spread by waterway, countrywide. Working the hard stone produced great amounts of waste; this eventually took over quarry production, and granite chippings, particularly useful for railway ballast, were made. This is a town for the industrial archaeologist, where granite and slate blend together by the former wharves of the canal – to the east of the village, the canalised river was heavily used for carrying stone, and wagon tipplers for loading up the boats can still be seen.

Coalville developed as a town from a railway station named Long Lane on the old Leicester-Swannington line (1832). The nearby coalmines were amongst the richest in the former Leicestershire coalfield, and it is not possible to think of Coalville without thinking of Desford Whitwick, Ellistown and Merry Lees, all pits in the Leicestershire coalfield which provided generations of miners with a living until the end arrived with the closure of Bagworth Colliery in 1991. Much of the evidence of coal mining has now disappeared from the area, but at Snibston, to the north-west of Coalville, a glimpse of mining life can be had at a museum of coal mining known as Snibston Discovery Museum near Coalville.

MOUNTSORREL, THE RIVER SOAR
c1960 M2363268

Some seven miles to the west of Coalville is Moira, developed as an industrial village in the early 19th century by the Irish Earls of Moira, who erected a smelting furnace here around 1805. The ironstone in the area turned out to be poor, which caused the furnace to close rather abruptly before 1815. The furnace (together with its adjacent cottages and associated kilns, which remain in situ) is a scheduled Ancient Monument, setting it alongside the Bedlam Furnace at Ironbridge.

Kirby Muxloe is famous for its ruined castle, seen in photograph K126004, below, set within a rectangular moat. Begun by William Hastings, 1st Lord Hastings of Ashby-de-la-Zouch, around 1480, but never finished, Kirby Muxloe is an early example of the use of brick in castle building. Although equipped with loops for handguns (they are the openings that look like inverted keyholes), Kirkby was intended to be more a fortified manor house than a fortress. The surviving west tower is where Jane Shore, mistress of Edward IV (1442-1483), came to live after the king's death.

KIRBY MUXLOE, THE CASTLE
c1965 K126004

GROBY, THE POOL c1960 G220007

The name of the village of Quorn was shortened from Quorndon in 1889, to avoid postal confusion with the name of the village of Quarndon, a few miles away. The village name was recorded as 'Querendon' in 1209, and the original name probably came from the Old English 'cweordun', meaning 'the hill where millstones are quarried.' Stone for millstones is known to have been quarried here in the Iron Age, and during the Roman period stone was taken from the local quarries to build Ratae Coritanorum (Roman Leicester). In the 19th century many villagers made their living as framework knitters, and terraced cottages in Sarson Street have the large windows which were a feature of their homes, allowing the knitters to work in as much light as possible.

Groby Pool, 4 miles north-west of Leicester, is seen in photograph G220007, above. Once it was larger, but its 40 acres qualified the pool as the largest sheet of water in the county until the 19th century, hence the Leicestershire saying 'to thatch Groby Pool with pancakes', which indicates any impossible undertaking.

Oakham is the county town of Rutland. The golden stone of the town's buildings enhances views along the High Street, and in particular the area around the market place. The surviving hall within the castle earthworks served as a local court room until 1970, with its famous collection of horseshoes occupying much of the wall space, each donated by peers of the realm on their first visits to the town.

Oakham was the birthplace of Sir Jeffrey Hudson (1619-1682), 'the shortest knight in the kingdom'. Known as 'The Rutland Dwarf', he was only 18 inches tall from the ages of eight to thirty. Later he grew to 3 feet 6 inches. When he was nine he was taken up to the Duke of Buckingham's mansion at Burley-on-the-Hill on the occasion of the visit of Charles I and his queen, Henrietta Maria, and as a dinner-time diversion he jumped out of a cold pie dressed in a tiny suit of armour. So impressed was the queen that she took Jeffrey into her service and had him knighted. He became a darling of the court, was made a captain of horse and had many adventures in his life, including being taken prisoner by pirates and nearly drowning in a wash basin!

OAKHAM, HIGH STREET 1927 80284

UPPINGHAM, THE MARKET PLACE 1932 85156

Uppingham is a particularly charming town with an attractive series of
17th and 18th-century buildings, and is also home to a famous public
school. During the 18th century the town was known for trades such
as building, quarrying (to provide ironstone for houses), leather, metal
and woodworking. Uppingham was well-known for its manufacture
of trenchers – large, round wooden plates – and 'as round as an
Uppingham trencher' was a popular saying.

Uppingham is surrounded by stone villages of outstanding quality.
To the south is Lyddington, with its wide main street and Bede House,
originally part of the Bishop of Lincoln's palace, now in the care of
English Heritage; a mile or so to its west is Stoke Dry, a single street
on a steep hill running down to Eye Brook Reservoir. Here is a church
where the Gunpowder Plotters are said to have met, with its strange
carving, wall paintings and Digby monuments. To the north of the
town, and almost in a line from east to west, are the stone villages of
Wing, with its mazes, Preston and Ridlington.

BELVOIR CASTLE, FROM THE AIR c1960 B633078

An aerial view of Belvoir Castle is shown in photograph B633078 (above). The first castle here was built by William the Conqueror's standard bearer, Robert de Todeni, on an escarpment rising above the surrounding countryside. By the mid 15th century the original castle was ruinous, but was rebuilt in the 16th century. Ruinous again by 1649, it was rebuilt at the wish of the Countess of Rutland by the pupil of Inigo Jones, Philip Webb. In 1801 the architect James Wyatt was engaged to remodel the building. Belvoir is the ideal castle of 19th-century romantic fiction, with its towers and crenellations breathing life into the Gothic fantasy world. The aerial photograph shows an apparently unstructured plan, but the castle is in fact roughly rectangular around a central courtyard.

It was at Belvoir Castle in Rutland that the ritual of afternoon teatime is said to have originated. Anna Maria Stanhope, the 7th Duchess of Bedford, was visiting Belvoir in the 1840s and found herself in need of extra sustenance to see her through the period from luncheon until the formal dinner in the evening. She asked the servants to bring tea-making equipment and some bread and butter discreetly to her room, and found this extra snack so enjoyable that she invited her friends to join her in the late afternoons to partake of a cup of tea with a dainty sandwich or a small cake. The Duchess continued the custom when she returned to London, and soon every fashionable hostess was following her lead.

St Mary's Church in Bottesford is famous for the magnificent series of monuments to the Roos family of the 15th century, and above all to eight Earls of Rutland, ranging from 1543 to 1679. The monument seen in photograph 22861, right, commemorates the 2nd Earl, who died in 1563. A lively tomb, it has the Earl and his wife lying under a domestic-looking table, upon which are kneeling figures and a vertical armorial slab.

**BOTTESFORD
ST MARY'S CHURCH
THE EARL OF
RUTLAND'S
MONUMENT 1890** 22861

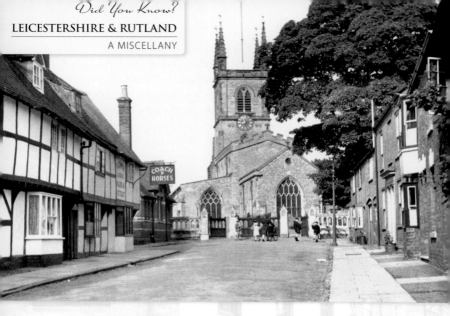

LUTTERWORTH, CHURCH STREET AND THE CHURCH c1955 L307002

Lutterworth is famous for its association with John Wycliff, a religious reformer and translator of the Bible into vernacular English, who was condemned by the Pope in 1377 for his attacks on clerical wealth and privileges. He is sometimes referred to as 'the Morning Star of the Reformation'. Wycliff came to Lutterworth as rector of the parish church, under the protection of John of Gaunt, and died there in 1384. Sadly, his remains were not to rest in peace, as they were exhumed and burnt in 1428, and the remnants thrown into the River Swift. The church in Lutterworth has a good white marble monument to Wycliff in the south aisle, by Richard Westmacott and dated 1837.

The town hall of Lutterworth was designed in 1836 by Joseph Aloysius Hansom, who is better known as the inventor of the hansom cab.

Photograph K171033 (below) shows the old mill at Kibworth Harcourt. Dated 1711, this last post-mill in the country ceased working in 1912. With its two pairs of stones, the design is such that the weather-boarded structure revolves round a central post, ensuring that the four great sails are always in the optimum position to take advantage of any available wind.

KIBWORTH HARCOURT, THE OLD MILL c1960 K171033

SPORTING LEICESTERSHIRE

The 1914 Grand National winner, Sunloch, came from Loughborough, and was owned by a local man, Thomas Tyler. The racehorse was trained in a field behind the Brush Works. From a 100-1 outsider a month before the race, the odds shortened dramatically as local people backed the horse. When it won, it was said that as much as £10,000 (then an enormous sum) was due to local punters in Loughborough.

Horse racing in the Leicester area goes back to 1603. Since then racing has taken place at various locations including Victoria Park, St Mary's Field, and the present course at Oadby. Highlights over the last 400 years include the first running of the Leicester Gold Cup in 1807, and Gordon Richards riding his first winner, Gay Lord, in 1921.

There has been a long tradition of boxing greats in Market Harborough: Reggie Mean, British Heavyweight Champion 1931-32, George Aldridge, British Middleweight Champion 1963-64, and Jack Gardner, who represented Great Britain in the 1948 London Olympics and reached the very height of his sport when he gained three major boxing titles to become the British, British Empire and European Heavyweight Boxing Champion. A hall at Harborough Leisure Centre is named after him.

Loughborough Town Football Club 2, Aston Villa 1 – that was the scoreline in 1894. Loughborough's star player was Albert Carnelly, who played wearing a cap – it was said that when he took off his cap, a goal was sure to follow. He transferred from Loughborough to Nottingham Forest FC in 1894.

Belgrave-born Jenny Fletcher was a star of women's swimming in the early 1900s. She was undefeated over four years from 1906-09, setting 11 new world records during this time. Her wins included 6 'Champion of England' medals, and an Olympic Gold Medal. She was inducted into the International Swimming Hall of Fame in 1971, with the inscription 'The World's First Great Woman Swimmer' above her picture.

Grace Road in Leicester is the home of Leicestershire County Cricket Club. They have played there since 1877, and the ground is said to have the second largest playing area in the world.

On 10 February 1923, England beat Ireland at rugby at Leicester's Welford Road ground. It was significant as being the last England home match played away from Twickenham until 1992, 69 years later. Another game played against Ireland, in 1984, saw seven Leicester players line up for their country, a club record.

A notable Leicester City FC record is that of goalkeeper Mark Wallington. He didn't miss a single match between 1975 and 1981. One of Leicester's most famous sporting sons is Gary Lineker, born in the city in 1960, who played for Leicester City for seven years before joining Everton in 1985. He made his England debut in May 1984 against Scotland at Hampden Park. He became the first England international to win the World Cup Golden Boot in the 1986 World Cup Finals, and went on to captain England from 1990-92. He finished his career as England's second highest goal scorer, his final score of 48 being only one goal behind the record holder, Bobby Charlton, and is famous for never having been booked.

The Sporting Success statue in Gallowtree Gate in Leicester commemorates that fact that Leicester teams in the sports of cricket, football and rugby each won a major trophy in 1996; representatives from all three sports are featured on the statue.

KIBWORTH BEAUCHAMP, THE CRICKET GROUND c1955 K119002

QUIZ QUESTIONS

Answers on page 52.

1. The Settling Rooms can be found in the middle of Sainsbury's car park in Market Harborough. How did the building get its name?

2. What is the connection between Leicester and the actor John Hurt?

3. How did the Magazine Gateway in Leicester get its name?

4. What fate might befall a nagging woman in Loughborough in the past?

5. What was the connection between Market Harborough and the Antarctic in 1901?

6. The popular singer Arnold George Dorsey grew up in Leicester. By what name is he better known?

7. What dreadful fate befell Nicholas Wollands in 16th-century Loughborough?

8. How did the 'Old English Gentleman' and the 'Generous Briton' public houses in Ashby Road in Loughborough get their names?

9. What is 'the Barrow Kipper', and where can you find it?

10. A tomb in a Leicestershire church may be the only grave in England showing an inscription blaming witchcraft for the deaths of its occupants. The church is shown below – where is it?

RECIPE

BEAN AND BACON BROTH

This recipe recalls the old saying 'Shake a Leicestershire yeoman, and you will hear the beans rattle in his belly', a reference to the staple diet of the county's agricultural labourers in former times. 'Bean-belly Leicestershire' was once a name given to the county, because of the extent to which beans were grown there.

2 tablespoonfuls oil
1 large onion, finely chopped
1 leek, trimmed, washed and chopped
1 garlic clove, crushed
4 streaky bacon rashers, rinded and chopped
2 tablespoonfuls plain flour
600ml/1 pint chicken or vegetable stock
115-175g/4-6oz dried butter or haricot beans, soaked overnight
    and rinsed (canned beans can also be used if preferred)
1 large tin of canned tomatoes
Salt and pepper
1 bay leaf
Chopped fresh parsley to garnish

Heat the oil in a saucepan and fry the onion until softened. Stir in the leek, garlic and bacon and fry gently for 5 minutes. Add the flour and stir well, then gradually stir in the stock. Bring to the boil. Drain the beans and add to the pan with the tomatoes, salt, pepper and bay leaf. Return to the boil, cover and simmer gently for about 1 hour or until the beans are tender. Discard the bay leaf, and serve sprinkled with chopped fresh parsley, accompanied with crusty bread.

OAKHAM, SHOP IN THE MARKET PLACE 1932 85151x

MARKET BOSWORTH, MARKET PLACE c1955   M233012

RECIPE

BOSWORTH JUMBLES

These small 'S'-shaped cakes were said to have been a speciality of Richard III's cook. King Richard was killed at the Battle of Bosworth, near Market Bosworth in Leicestershire, in 1485 when his forces were defeated by the army of Henry VII. There is an old story that the recipe for Bosworth Jumbles was found on the battlefield! The site of the battle is open to the public, and is well exhibited. In former times jumbles were made in the form of two interlaced rings – their name derives from the word 'gemmel' for a twin finger ring.

225g/8oz self-raising flour
175g/6oz butter or margarine
175g/6oz caster sugar
1 egg, beaten
1 teaspoonful finely grated lemon rind
Half a teaspoonful almond essence (optional)

Pre-heat the oven to 180°C/350°F/Gas Mark 4. Cream the butter or margarine with the sugar until it is light and fluffy. Carefully beat in the egg, a little at a time, and the lemon rind and almond essence, if used. Gradually mix in the sieved flour, and mix it all to a stiff consistency. Take small pieces of the dough, roll them lightly in your hands and form the pieces into 'S' shapes.

Place the jumbles on greased and floured baking sheets, well spaced out so that they will not run together while baking. Bake in the pre-heated oven for about 10-15 minutes, giving them a quarter turn after 5-7 minutes so that they all bake evenly.

QUIZ ANSWERS

1. The Settling Rooms is all that remains of Market Harborough's purpose-built livestock market site of 1903. On market days the building was used for settling up payments after the auctioneer had completed the selling of livestock.

2. 50 Lee Street in Leicester was the birthplace in 1862 of Joseph Merrick, better known as the tragic Elephant Man, who was played by John Hurt in a film about Merrick's life.

3. The Magazine Gateway in Leicester should really be called the Newarke Gateway, as it was the entrance to the Newarke, a 14th-century addition to Leicester Castle. However it gained the name Magazine Gateway during the Civil War, when it was used to store the town's 'magazine' – its supply of weapons and gunpowder.

4. Women in Loughborough in the past who were judged to be scolds or foul-mouthed were sentenced to the 'cucke stool'. After being bound in this armchair-like apparatus, offenders were paraded round the town and then taken to the river near Cotes Mill, where the unfortunate woman was dunked in the river.

5. The Market Harborough company W Symington received a great publicity boost in 1901 when the famous explorer Captain Scott commissioned the firm to supply its pea flour and pea soup as part of his supplies for his first Antarctic expedition (1901-1904). Fifty years later one of Scott's food stores was discovered, and the pea flour was found to still be in perfect condition.

6. Arnold George Dorsey is better known as Engelbert Humperdinck. Of Anglo Indian ethnicity, he was born on 2 May 1936 in what was then known as Madras, India, and was raised in Leicester. He adopted the stage name Engelbert Humperdinck, after the German opera composer of the same name.

7. When an animal menagerie visited Loughborough during Elizabethan times, amongst the exhibits to be seen was a lioness. Townsman Nicholas Wollands was attacked by the beast and was 'sore wounded in sundry places'. The injuries sadly proved fatal.

8. The 'Old English Gentleman' and the 'Generous Briton' public houses in Ashby Road in Loughborough were probably named after King William IV, who reigned from 1830 to 1837. He was popular with brewers and drinkers because he helped to ensure that taxation on beer was reduced.

9. The village of Barrow-upon-Soar, about eight miles north of Leicester, is famous for its limeworks. In 1851 the fossilised remains of a plesiosaur were found in a lime pit here; nicknamed the 'Barrow Kipper', it can now be seen in the Leicestershire Museum and Art Gallery in Leicester, and is commemorated on the village sign at a roundabout at the entrance to the village (see photograph B514025x, below).

10. In St Mary's Church in Bottesford. The inscription records that the two sons of Francis, 6th Earl of Rutland 'dyed in their infancy by wicked practice and sorcery'. The deaths were blamed on the six Witches of Belvoir, led by Joan Flower, whose daughter Margaret had worked at the manor house until she was dismissed for stealing; Joan and her fellow witches were believed to have taken revenge by killing the young boys with black magic. When she was tried, Joan demanded a piece of bread to eat, saying that it would choke her if she was guilty – and promptly fell down dead in court. The other five witches then admitted practicing black magic, and were hanged at Lincoln in 1619.

BARROW-UPON-SOAR, THE VILLAGE SIGN c1965 B514025x

FRANCIS FRITH

PIONEER VICTORIAN PHOTOGRAPHER

Francis Frith, founder of the world-famous photographic archive, was a complex and multi-talented man. A devout Quaker and a highly successful Victorian businessman, he was philosophical by nature and pioneering in outlook. By 1855 he had already established a wholesale grocery business in Liverpool, and sold it for the astonishing sum of £200,000, which is the equivalent today of over £15,000,000. Now in his thirties, and captivated by the new science of photography, Frith set out on a series of pioneering journeys up the Nile and to the Near East.

INTRIGUE AND EXPLORATION

He was the first photographer to venture beyond the sixth cataract of the Nile. Africa was still the mysterious 'Dark Continent', and Stanley and Livingstone's historic meeting was a decade into the future. The conditions for picture taking confound belief. He laboured for hours in his wicker dark-room in the sweltering heat of the desert, while the volatile chemicals fizzed dangerously in their trays. Back in London he exhibited his photographs and was 'rapturously cheered' by members of the Royal Society. His reputation as a photographer was made overnight.

VENTURE OF A LIFE-TIME

By the 1870s the railways had threaded their way across the country, and Bank Holidays and half-day Saturdays had been made obligatory by Act of Parliament. All of a sudden the working man and his family were able to enjoy days out, take holidays, and see a little more of the world.

With typical business acumen, Francis Frith foresaw that these new tourists would enjoy having souvenirs to commemorate their days out. For the next thirty years he travelled the country by train and by pony and trap, producing fine photographs of seaside resorts and beauty spots that were keenly bought by millions of Victorians. These prints were painstakingly pasted into family albums and pored over during the dark nights of winter, rekindling precious memories of summer excursions. Frith's studio was soon supplying retail shops all over the country, and by 1890 F Frith & Co had become the greatest specialist photographic publishing company in the world, with over 2,000 sales outlets, and pioneered the picture postcard.

FRANCIS FRITH'S LEGACY

Francis Frith had died in 1898 at his villa in Cannes, his great project still growing. By 1970 the archive he created contained over a third of a million pictures showing 7,000 British towns and villages.

Frith's legacy to us today is of immense significance and value, for the magnificent archive of evocative photographs he created provides a unique record of change in the cities, towns and villages throughout Britain over a century and more. Frith and his fellow studio photographers revisited locations many times down the years to update their views, compiling for us an enthralling and colourful pageant of British life and character.

We are fortunate that Frith was dedicated to recording the minutiae of everyday life. For it is this sheer wealth of visual data, the painstaking chronicle of changes in dress, transport, street layouts, buildings, housing and landscape that captivates us so much today, offering us a powerful link with the past and with the lives of our ancestors.

Computers have now made it possible for Frith's many thousands of images to be accessed almost instantly. The archive offers every one of us an opportunity to examine the places where we and our families have lived and worked down the years. Its images, depicting our shared past, are now bringing pleasure and enlightenment to millions around the world a century and more after his death.

For further information visit: www.francisfrith.com

INTERIOR DECORATION

Frith's photographs can be seen framed and as giant wall murals in thousands of pubs, restaurants, hotels, banks, retail stores and other public buildings throughout Britain. These provide interesting and attractive décor, generating strong local interest and acting as a powerful reminder of gentler days in our increasingly busy and frenetic world.

FRITH PRODUCTS

All Frith photographs are available as prints and posters in a variety of different sizes and styles. In the UK we also offer a range of other gift and stationery products illustrated with Frith photographs, although many of these are not available for delivery outside the UK – see our web site for more information on the products available for delivery in your country.

THE INTERNET

Over 100,000 photographs of Britain can be viewed and purchased on the Frith web site. The web site also includes memories and reminiscences contributed by our customers, who have personal knowledge of localities and of the people and properties depicted in Frith photographs. If you wish to learn more about a specific town or village you may find these reminiscences fascinating to browse. Why not add your own comments if you think they would be of interest to others? See **www.francisfrith.com**

PLEASE HELP US BRING FRITH'S PHOTOGRAPHS TO LIFE

Our authors do their best to recount the history of the places they write about. They give insights into how particular towns and villages developed, they describe the architecture of streets and buildings, and they discuss the lives of famous people who lived there. But however knowledgeable our authors are, the story they tell is necessarily incomplete.

Frith's photographs are so much more than plain historical documents. They are living proofs of the flow of human life down the generations. They show real people at real moments in history; and each of those people is the son or daughter of someone, the brother or sister, aunt or uncle, grandfather or grandmother of someone else. All of them lived, worked and played in the streets depicted in Frith's photographs.

We would be grateful if you would give us your insights into the places shown in our photographs: the streets and buildings, the shops, businesses and industries. Post your memories of life in those streets on the Frith website: what it was like growing up there, who ran the local shop and what shopping was like years ago; if your workplace is shown tell us about your working day and what the building is used for now. Read other visitors' memories and reconnect with your shared local history and heritage. With your help more and more Frith photographs can be brought to life, and vital memories preserved for posterity, and for the benefit of historians in the future.

Wherever possible, we will try to include some of your comments in future editions of our books. Moreover, if you spot errors in dates, titles or other facts, please let us know, because our archive records are not always completely accurate—they rely on 140 years of human endeavour and hand-compiled records. You can email us using the contact form on the website.

Thank you!

For further information, trade, or author enquiries
please contact us at the address below:

**The Francis Frith Collection, Oakley Business Park,
Wylye Road, Dinton, Wiltshire SP3 5EU.**
Tel: +44 (0)1722 716 376 Fax: +44 (0)1722 716 881
e-mail: sales@francisfrith.co.uk **www.francisfrith.com**